OLD WEST HISTORY

for Kids

Settlement of the American West (Wild West)

US Western History
6th Grade Social Studies

In this book, we're going to talk about the settlement of the America West. So, let's get right to it!

THE MISSISSIPPI RIVER

When the first settlers came to the United States, they settled along the eastern coastline. However, as the population grew, pioneers began to move west. The Mississippi River was a geographic dividing line that split the east from the west.

Eventually, adventurous Americans began to travel west of the river and settle in the regions of the Midwest and far West. Most of this expansion happened during the last part of the 19th century, but there were earlier events that pointed to what was to come.

SETTLERS AND THEIR TENTS
MESS CHEST
D.A.J.

OLD WESTERN STREET REPLICA

EARLY EXPANSION

By the year 1700, there were a quarter of a million people settled in the British colonies. Seventy-five years later, this growing population had reached over 2 million people. Many settlers were getting tired of the crowded areas in the east.

They wanted the freedom of open land to claim as their own for both farming and hunting. They began to move west of the Appalachian Mountains. One of the first regions where the settlers moved was described as the Northwest Territory.

APPALACHIAN MOUNTAINS

DANIEL BOONE

Today, this region is composed of the states of Illinois, Indiana, and Ohio as well as the states of Wisconsin and Michigan. The now-famous frontiersman Daniel Boone helped settlers travel through the Cumberland

Gap, a narrow passageway within the Appalachian Mountains near the location of the present-day states of Kentucky and Tennessee.

BOONE AT CUMBERLAND GAP

THE LOUISIANA PURCHASE

It didn't take long for the Northwest Territory to get crowded. Americans were hungry for more land. In the year 1803, Thomas Jefferson, the third president of the United States, negotiated with the French to buy the Louisiana Territory.

LOUISIANA PURCHASE, 1803

NAPOLEON BONAPARTE

At the beginning it was Jefferson's goal to buy the seaport of New Orleans. This major seaport was important to the United States since it was part of the Mississippi River system. The French ruler at that time was Napoleon Bonaparte.

At the start, Napoleon wasn't interested in selling, but soon he began to have financial troubles. He saw that he could ease his money problems by selling the Louisiana Territory to the United States. He eventually sold the huge piece of property to the United States government for $15 million.

FIRST RAISING OF THE USA FLAG
AFTER THE LOUISIANA PURCHASE

PORTRAIT OF MERIWEATHER LEWIS AND WILLIAM CLARK

Jefferson soon commissioned the explorers Lewis and Clark to determine the boundaries of this new acquisition, which had

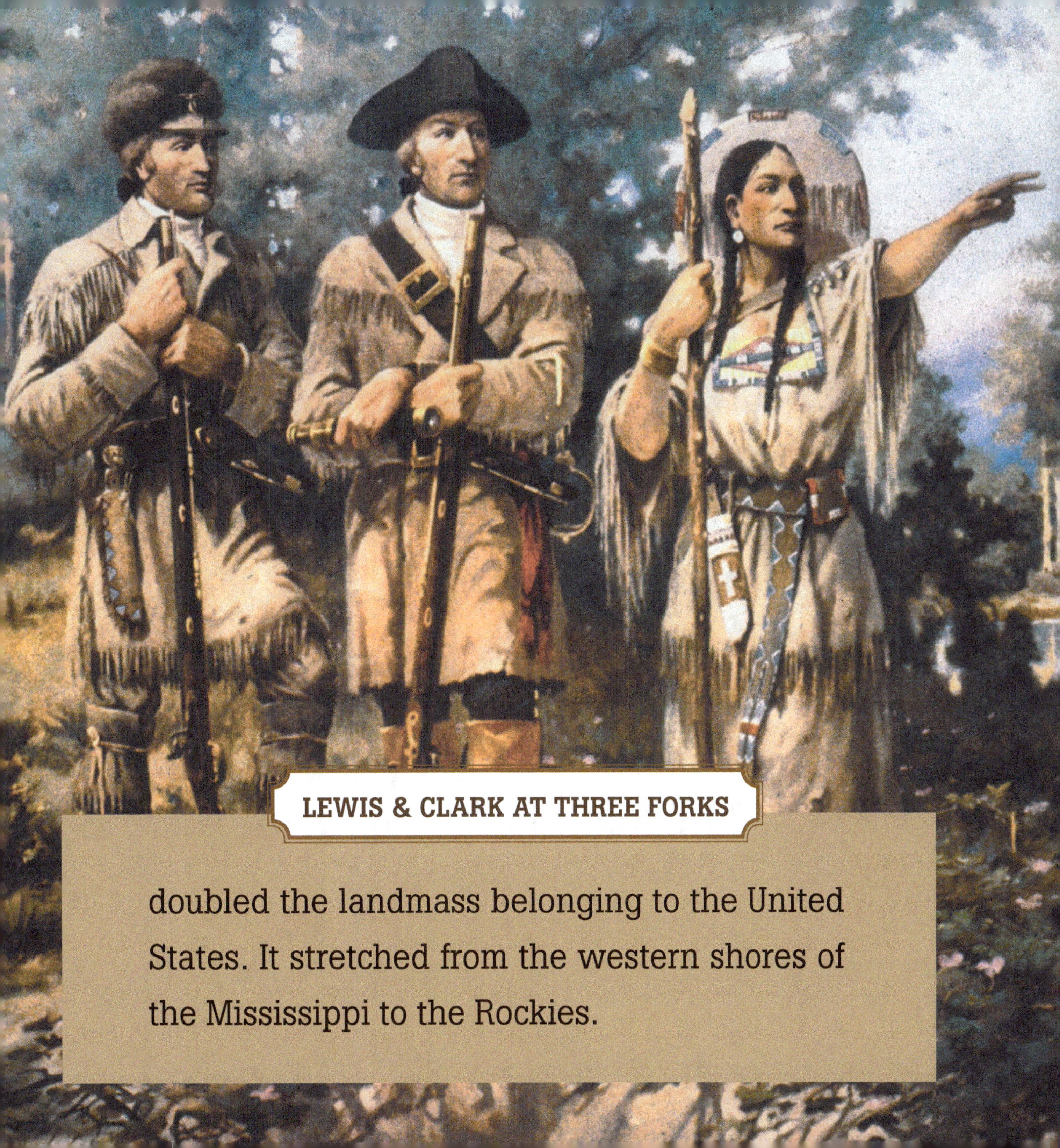

doubled the landmass belonging to the United States. It stretched from the western shores of the Mississippi to the Rockies.

t its south was the port of New Orleans and to its north was the region now composed of the states of Montana, North Dakota, and Minnesota. Jefferson was a firm believer that America should expand west and his acquisition of the Louisiana Territory was the first of many acquisitions that led America to expand all the way to the Pacific Coast.

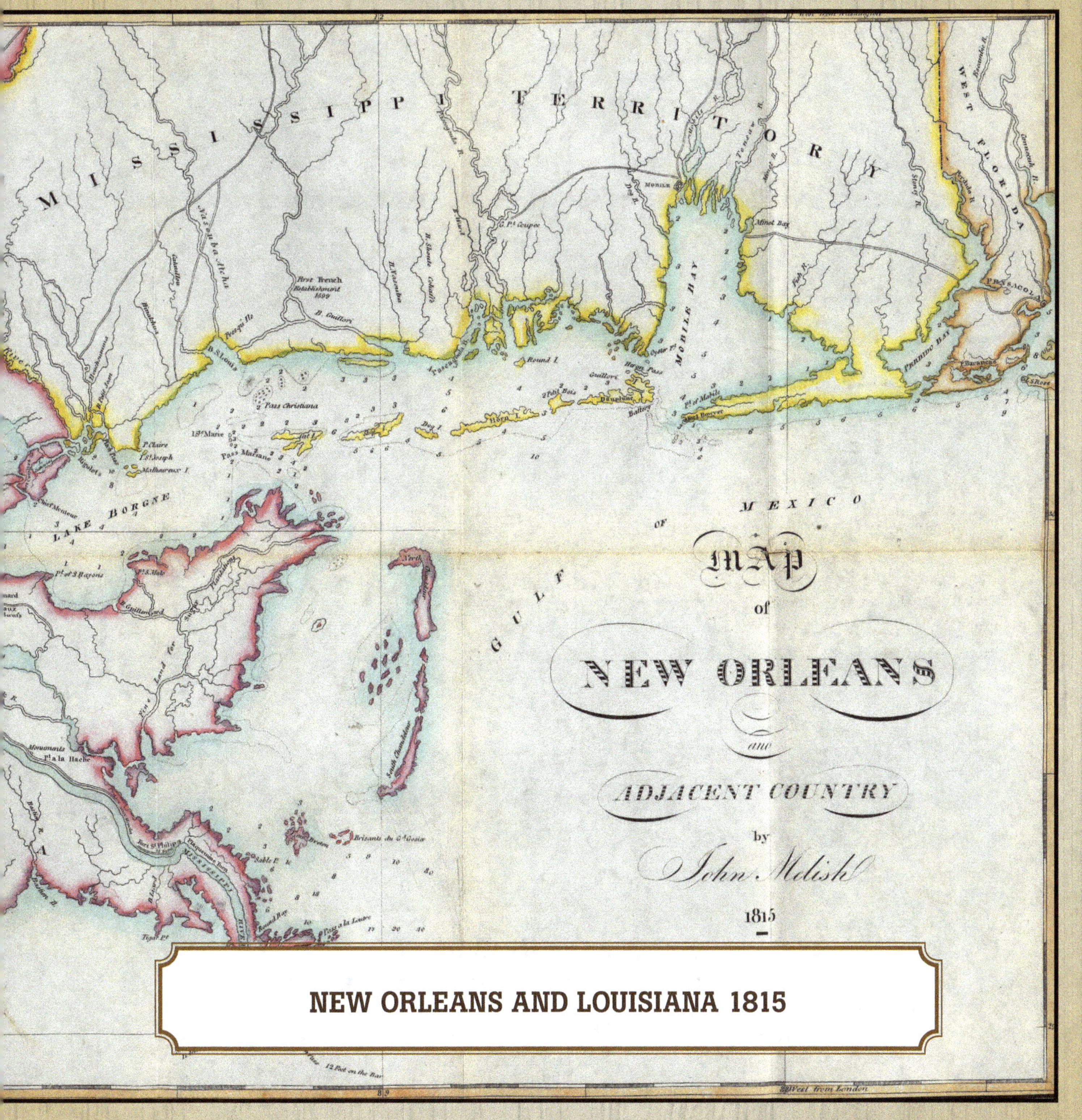

NEW ORLEANS AND LOUISIANA 1815

BATTLE OF CHURUBUSCO

THE MEXICAN–AMERICAN WAR

In 1821, Mexico had become independent from its parent country of Spain. Settlers began to move into Texas, which at that time was land that belonged to Mexico. The Texans began to fight with Mexico's government in an effort to become independent.

In the year 1836, they declared themselves to be an independent republic. After several battles, they were able to separate themselves from Mexico. In the year 1845, after some debate, they became part of the United States. There was tension between Mexico and the United States over the US acquisition of Texas. There were also disagreements related to the borders between the two countries.

WINGED VICTORY OR ANGEL OF INDEPENDENCE
IN THE ZOCALO OF MEXICO CITY

In the year 1846, the United States and Mexico went to war. Mexico lost the war and they also lost over 40% of their land in the process. The treaty at the end of the war made it possible for the United States to buy a large portion of land from Mexico for $15 million, the same price they

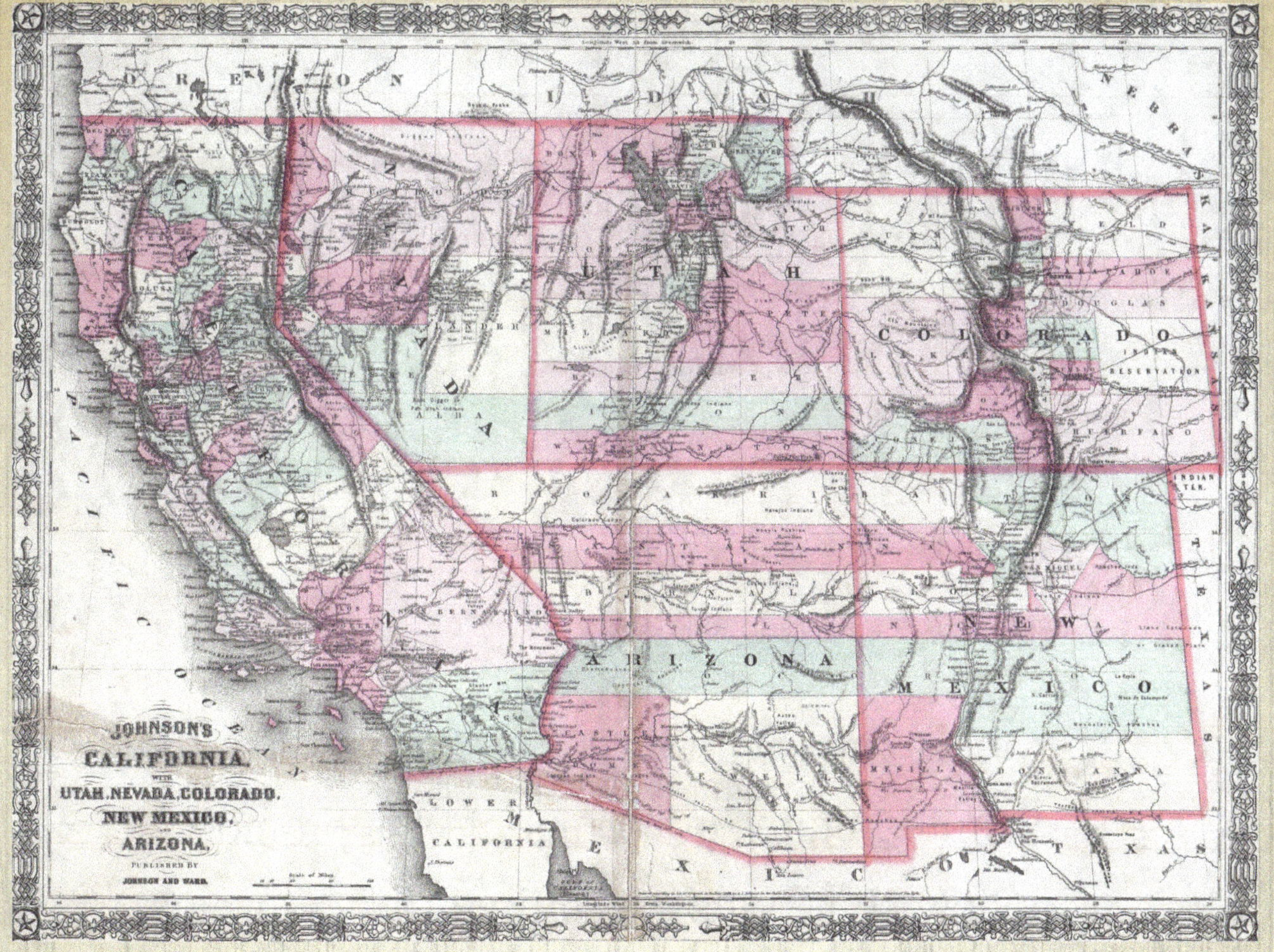

**1864 JOHNSON MAP OF CALIFORNIA,
NEVADA, UTAH, ARIZONA, NEW MEXICO**

had paid for the Louisiana Purchase. Today, that land is composed of four different states—Arizona, Utah, Nevada, and California. Portions of four other states were included in the land that Mexico sold as well.

WHAT WAS MANIFEST DESTINY?

Before the Civil War broke out in 1861, the United States government was promoting a policy that was described as "Manifest Destiny." This policy essentially said that it was appropriate for Americans to establish homes and farms on the lands west of the Mississippi.

UNITED STATES MISSISSIPPI GUN-BOATS BEING BUILT AT CARONDELET, NEAR ST. LOUIS, MISSOURI.
[Sketched by Alexander Simplot.]

It was considered their divine destiny to do so. This region of land is enormous since it encompassed all the land west of the Mississippi River to the Pacific coast.

UNDERTAKER
CHEAP ROOMS

WHY WAS IT CALLED THE WILD WEST?

It wasn't easy for the pioneers to claim and settle the lands in the West. It was wild territory and many pioneers died due to disease and the hardship of the journey.

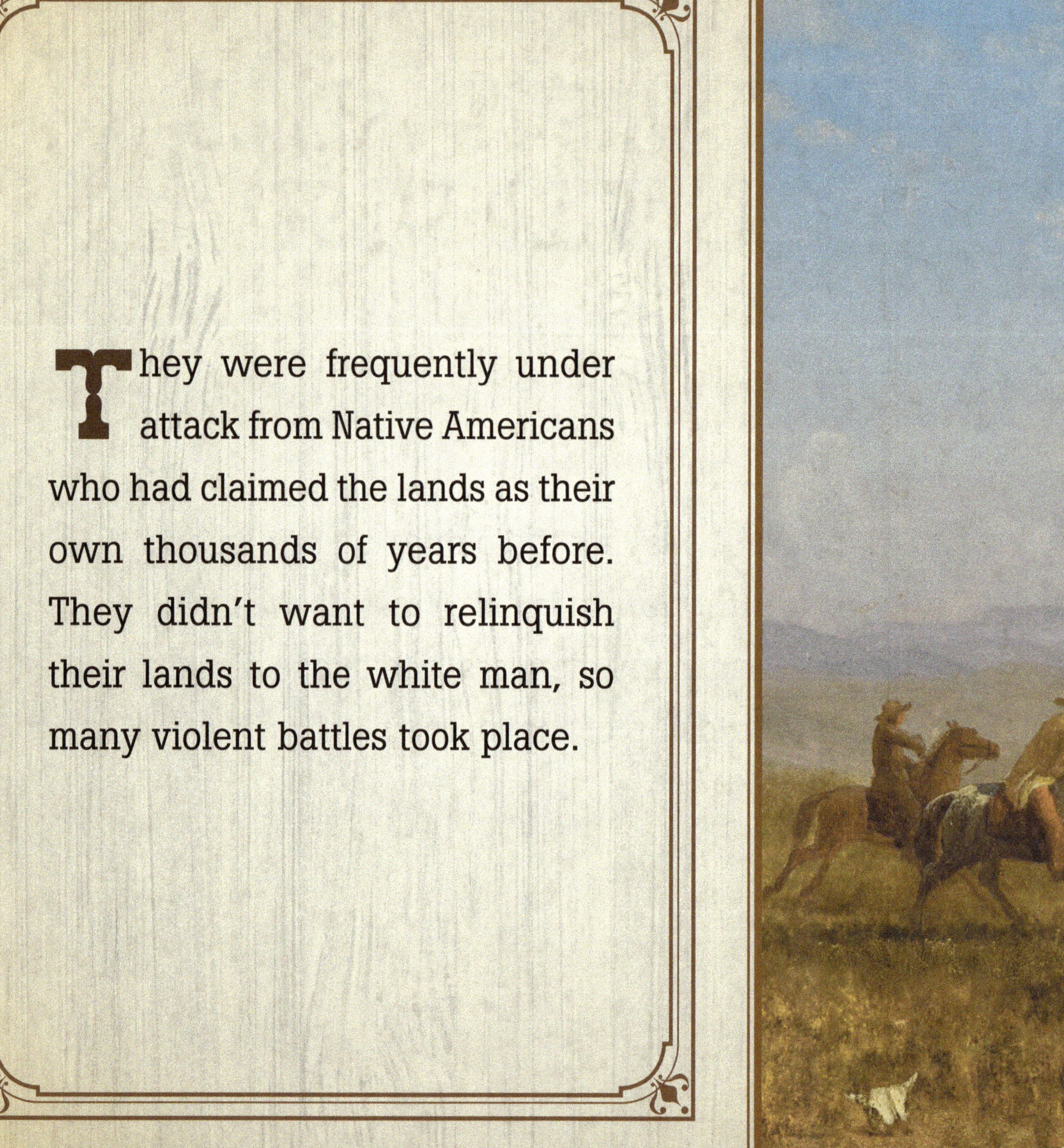

They were frequently under attack from Native Americans who had claimed the lands as their own thousands of years before. They didn't want to relinquish their lands to the white man, so many violent battles took place.

BUFFALO HUNTING

WILD WEST SHOW AT HIGH CHAPARRAL

The culture of the early days of the West was marked by violence and lawlessness. It was a daily struggle just to survive. There was constant tension between the Native Americans and the settlers.

This tension led to the Indian Wars and both sides had many casualties. Populations of some of the Native American tribes were completely wiped out.

The pioneers developed a Wild West philosophy. They claimed the lands they wanted and defended their property with guns and rifles. The Constitution guaranteed that they could bear arms so they weren't shy about bearing firearms and using them if anyone threatened their homes, farms, or ranches.

GUNFIGHTER OF THE WILD WEST AT THE TRAIN STATION

The last "line-up"—This remarkable picture, taken at roll-call, on Saturday afternoon, October 26, 1907, by Mrs. J. N. Watson wife of the Register of the United States Land Office at Lakeview, Oregon, is a faithful representation of the rush to secure claims whenever a large body of Government land is thrown open to public entry, and marks the last event of its kind of any moment, that will probably ever occur in Oregon.   About 40,000 acres that had been segregated from a forest reserve in the Lakeview Land District were restored to settlement Sept. 27, 1907, and opened to entry on the 27th of the following month.   Three weeks before the opening applicants commenced to line up at the local land office, and the number increased daily until the opening day, when 224 were in line

HOMESTEAD ACT 05

WHY DID THE PIONEERS WANT TO COME WEST?

There were many different reasons that the first pioneers wanted to travel to the West. The government had issued the Homestead Act, which meant that they could grab up lands for free to set up farms and ranches.

uring the Gold Rush in 1848, thousands of people flocked to California to see if they could "strike it rich."

nother reason that people came out West was for freedom from religious persecution.

THE OREGON TRAIL

HOW DID THE PIONEERS GET OUT WEST?

Beginning around 1811, fur trappers and traders built a trail that could be walked or traversed by horseback. It was known as the Oregon Trail. Eventually, the trail was cleared for use by wagons. Its starting point was the city of Independence in Missouri.

The trail was over 2,000 miles long and went through territory that today makes up six different states. The final destination of the trail was the town of Oregon City in the

state of Oregon. The terrain was very difficult and the travelers encountered many dangers. Two mountain ranges were in their path—the Rockies and the Sierra Nevada range.

CONESTOGA WAGON ON OREGON TRAIL

At that time, there were no cars or coast-to-coast railroads. In order to take their belongings, the pioneers traveled in wagons that were covered. The wagons were constructed of wood and braced with iron around their wheels.

The covers were built with cotton that was waterproofed or canvas made from linen cloth. A wagon that was loaded with people and possessions might weigh as much as 2,500 pounds. The covered wagons were called "Prairie Schooners" because they were similar to boats as they traveled across the vast expanses of flat prairie lands.

PRAIRIE SCHOONERS

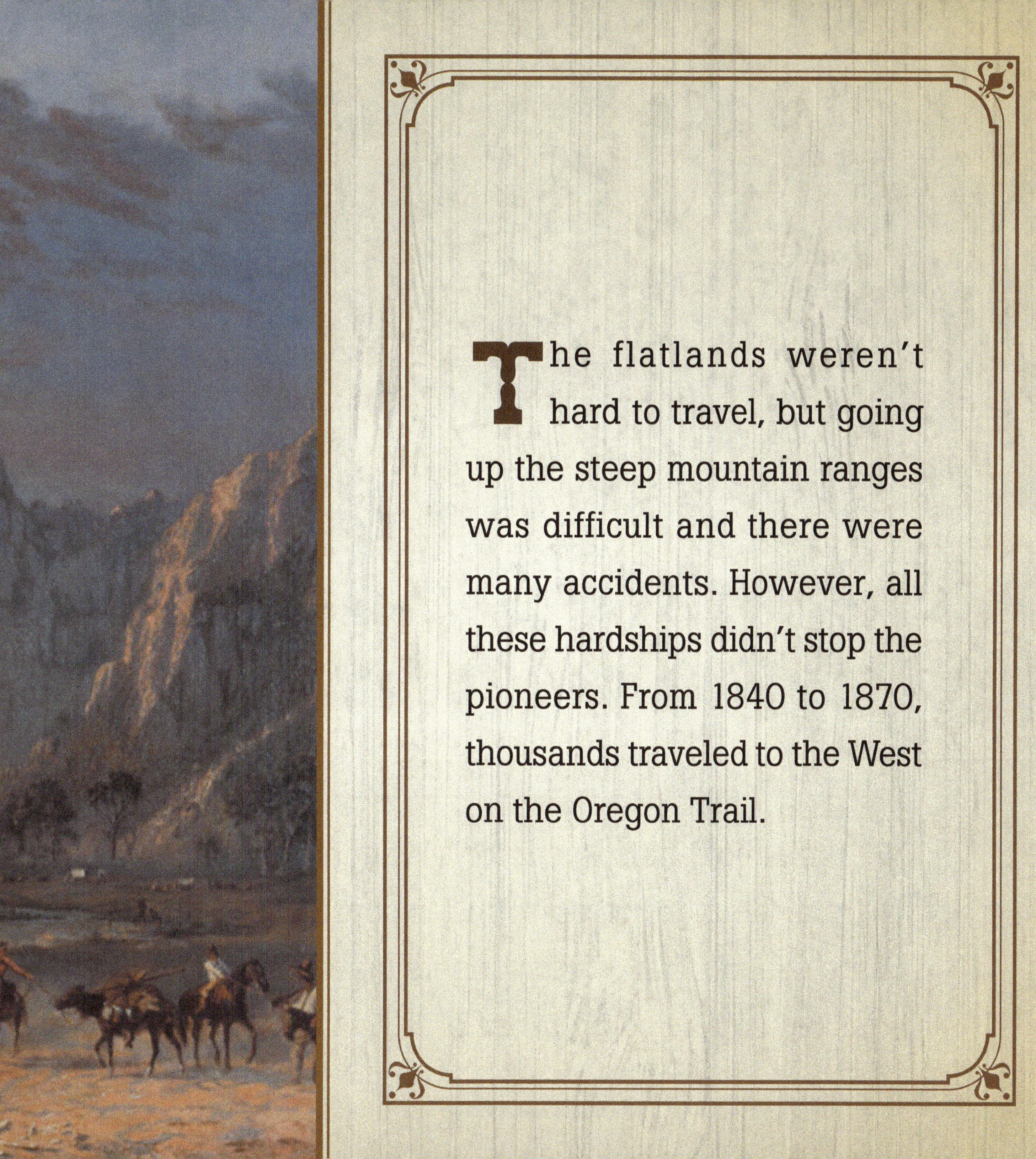

The flatlands weren't hard to travel, but going up the steep mountain ranges was difficult and there were many accidents. However, all these hardships didn't stop the pioneers. From 1840 to 1870, thousands traveled to the West on the Oregon Trail.

It took about half a year for a wagon train to get from the starting point in Missouri to the end of the Oregon Trail. The pioneers were sometimes attacked and killed by tribes of Native Americans.

However, not all the Native Americans they encountered were violent. In fact, some of them acted as guides and assisted them along the way.

When they left their homes in the east, the pioneers couldn't take many of their possessions. They only had a few articles of clothing, guns, and candles for light. Most of what they packed was food. They carried foods that were preserved, such as bacon and beans. They also took a few cooking implements such as coffee pots and iron skillets. About one thousand pounds of food had to be packed into the wagon for a family of two parents and two children to survive as they traveled out west.

SUMMARY

Americans weren't satisfied with populating the east coast. Eventually, they wanted to move out to the west where there was lots of open land to build their farms and ranches. The Gold Rush also provided a reason to head out West. For a long time, the West was very wild and lawless. The pioneers endured many hardships, such as disease and battles with Native Americans, as they traveled by covered wagon to settle in the West.

WANTED
REWARD
5.000

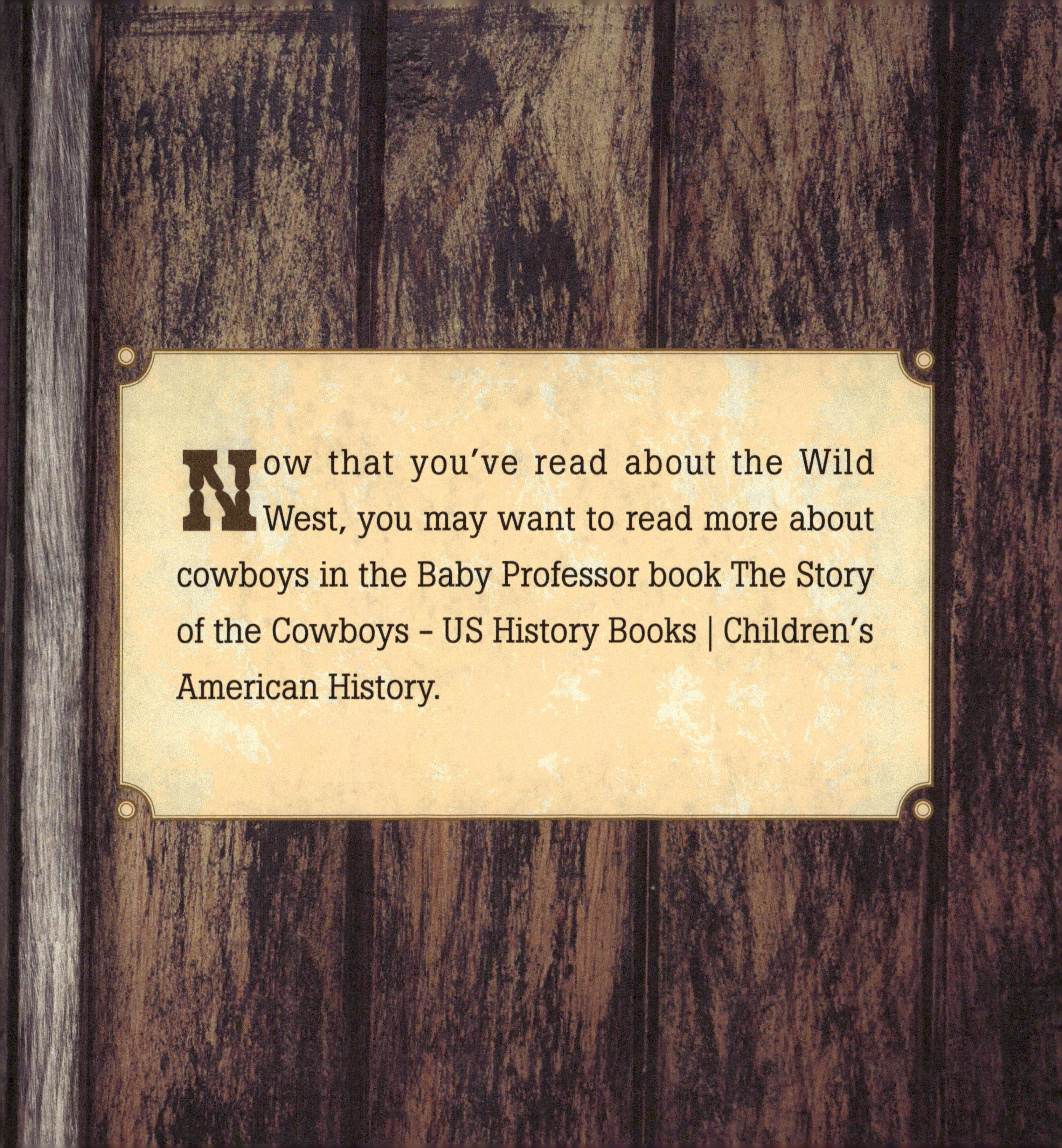

Now that you've read about the Wild West, you may want to read more about cowboys in the Baby Professor book The Story of the Cowboys – US History Books | Children's American History.

Visit

BABY PROFESSOR
EDUCATION KIDS

www.BabyProfessorBooks.com
to download Free Baby Professor eBooks
and view our catalog of new and exciting
Children's Books